394.2
LAS

Lasky, Kathryn.

Days of the Dead.

$16.49

452871

DATE			

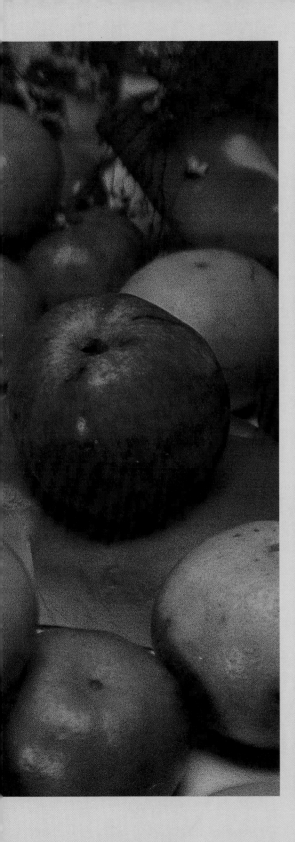

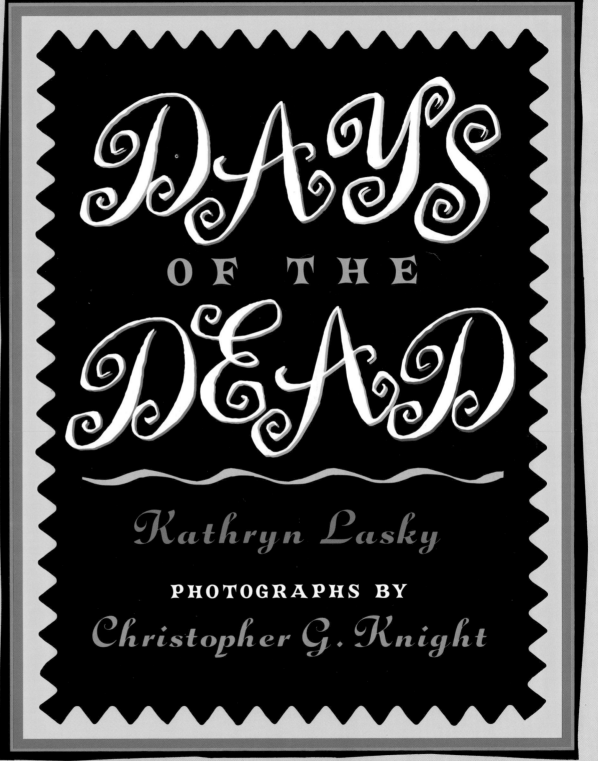

DAYS OF THE DEAD

Kathryn Lasky

PHOTOGRAPHS BY

Christopher G. Knight

HYPERION BOOKS FOR CHILDREN • NEW YORK

For information address
Hyperion Books for Children,
114 Fifth Avenue, New York, New York 10011.

FIRST EDITION
1 3 5 7 9 10 8 6 4 2

Lasky, Kathryn.
Days of the Dead/Kathryn Lasky;
photographs by Christopher G. Knight–1st ed.
p. cm.
ISBN 0-7868-0022-4 (trade)–ISBN 0-7868-2018-7 (lib. bdg.)
1. All Souls' Day–Mexico–Juvenile literature.
2. All Saints' Day–Mexico–Juvenile literature.
3. Mexico–Social life and customs–Juvenile literature.
I. Knight, Christopher G. II. Title.
GT4995.A4L37 1994
394.2'64–dc20 93-47957 CIP AC

This book is set in 14-point Barcelona Book.

nto a valley deep in the heart of Mexico, nearly half a century ago, came a young man named Juan de Jesús and his wife, Domatilla. They walked, the man leading a burro and the woman carrying a small infant wrapped in her *rebozo,* a shawl. They came to search for land to farm and a good place to raise their family. They liked the valley. The soil seemed rich, and they hoped the winters would not be too harsh or the summers too dry. So they settled there, first building a small one-room log house, then another cabin just for cooking and a few stalls for animals. They raised sheep and chickens and turkeys, and grew vegetables. They would have five more children.

Even after Domatilla and Juan died, some of their children and grandchildren continued to live on the small farm in the valley. Others moved higher into the hills, and some moved to Mexico City. But on the second to last day in the month of October, many of them are coming back to the valley and to the home that Juan and Domatilla built. For it is *los Dias de Muertos,* the Days of the Dead, and the children and grandchildren have returned to welcome their grandparents' spirits home.

7

*L*os Días de Muertos is a traditional holiday in Mexico that honors the dead. Throughout the country Mexicans are preparing to welcome the spirits of their departed ancestors and friends. People stream into the cemeteries with flowers, wash buckets, scrub brushes, and hoes to begin cleaning up the graves, *las tumbas.* When the graves are scrubbed and the flowers arranged, candles will be lit for the returning spirits of the autumn night.

These days are not sad. The crying is over, and now is the time for remembering and rejoicing and even for mocking death. In the towns boisterous high school students are dressed as ghouls and mummies and monsters. They shout, *"¡Calaveras! ¡Calaveras!"* (Skulls! Skulls!) as they make their raucous way through the narrow streets of a hill town. It is almost as if they were saying trick or treat because they are asking for sweets and fruit and money.

They carry a coffin and in it is a smiling "corpse" who especially likes oranges and gives a cheer every time a market vendor throws one into the casket. A lucky corpse can catch bunches of flowers, fruits, and candy.

Shop windows display *calacas*, the handmade figurines that show a lively afterlife where skeleton musicians continue to play in jazz bands, writers tap their bony fingers on typewriters, and even brides in dresses as white as their bones march down the aisle with skeleton grooms.

Bakers' trays are filled with chocolate and sugar skulls, marzipan coffins, and white chocolate skeletons. There are special loaves of bread, *pan de muertos,* with "bones" decorating the crust. There are candles for sale, and the markets are crammed with flowers.

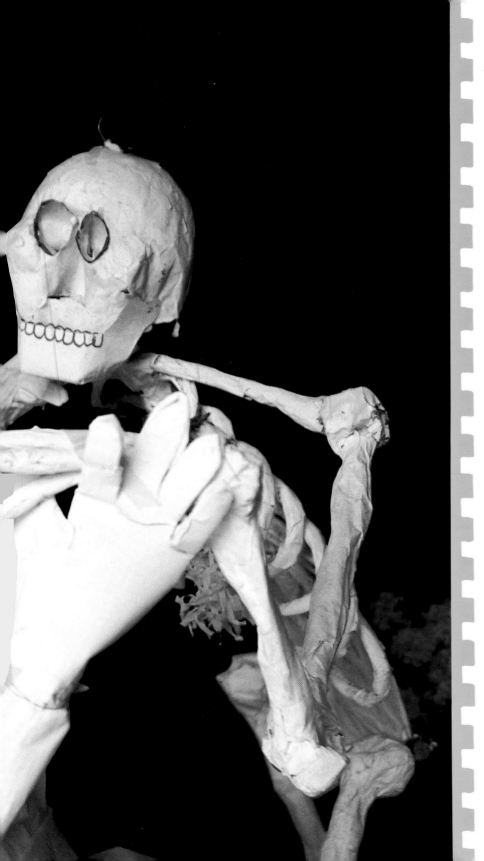

At a roadside, in a small fenced enclosure, a woman is busy arranging flowers in vases. This is the spot where her brother and his friend died in a car crash. At night she will place a candle there to beckon the spirits, and then, beyond the highway, near the doorway to her house in the village, she will lay a path of marigold petals to guide the spirits to her kitchen. There she has spread a table with beautiful flowers and set out their favorite foods.

Autumn is a time of dying, of preparing for winter's sleep, and celebrations of death come at this time of year in many cultures and religions. Halloween grew out of the Celtic festival Samhain, celebrating the passing of summer and the arrival of winter. The Celts believed that during this festival the souls of the dead were allowed to return to their earthly homes for the evening. The ancient Egyptians also celebrated death. Osiris, god of vegetation and thought to be the ruler who granted life from the underworld as well as immortality, was remembered every year in November, the time when the Nile was annually sinking and when it was believed he had drowned. Ancient Egyptians believed that life did not end with death and that at this time of year the dead returned to visit their homes, so lamps were lit to show the way.

The Aztec people of Mexico did not fear death. Though life on earth was harsh, they envisioned an afterlife where warriors and children became hummingbirds and butterflies, where infants who had died at birth suckled at a heavenly nursing tree, where the dead were never judged but lived in eternal happiness, and where life was seen only as a brief dream on the way to death, the only reality.

But in Mexico, autumn also brings signs of rebirth. Between the wet and the dry seasons, the countryside bursts with blooming flowers: great waves of golden-eyed sunflowers, white daisies, red poinsettias, and purple salvias. The monarch butterflies that have summered in the north return south to winter in the protection of the *oyamel* fir forests.

It is always around the Days of the Dead that the butterflies' silhouettes are first spotted. They have flown thousands of miles, some from as far as Canada. The rivulets of butterflies streaming in from the northeast will become thicker and thicker until they are like sparkling streams in the skies. The monarchs embroider the air with their orange-and-black finery as they glide on gossamer-thin wings to their roosting places in the trees. There they cluster on branches in immense bunches looking like tissue-paper shingles. In one forest near the de Jesús family's house it has been estimated that there are over thirty million butterflies.

Evidence that butterflies have been linked with the spirits of the dead since ancient times is found in the monarch images carved in stone on many Aztec monuments. Throughout the centuries the inhabitants of Mexico have believed that the returning butterflies bear the spirits of the departed.

$\mathcal{S}$he does not need the marigold path. *Abuela,* my grandmother, knows the way. She took the sheep very far, and she could always find a lost one even behind the mountain. She will find our *ofrenda* and so will *Abuelo.*"

Gamaliel is twelve years old. He remembers his grandparents well, especially his grandmother Domatilla, for together they herded the sheep. They would leave early in the morning, when the frost silvered the meadow, to take sheep far into the back country, where they could gather kindling and wood for their fire.

Gamaliel's little sister Noemi always begs to go with her big brother. But she is not much help. She is not big enough to pick up a stubborn sheep and carry it back to where it is supposed to be grazing, and she doesn't run fast enough to head off the herd if it decides to graze in a neighbor's garden on the way to the meadow.

17

Gamaliel and his brothers and sisters and cousins must haul water from a spring almost half a mile away. They feed the chickens and guard the turkeys, for coyotes love turkey as well as lamb. Gamaliel checks up on the baby burro in the lower pasture. Much of this must be done before breakfast. There is a lot of work for him to do on the farm because his father and older brother work most of the time in Mexico City, where the pay is better, and Gamaliel is the oldest child at home.

On the farm, work and play get mixed up together. But there is no time or money for school. Gamaliel had to quit after sixth grade. The school that he would go to for seventh grade was twelve miles away, and his parents could not afford the cost of the bus ride.

There is no electricity in Gamaliel's house. In the cooking house, which is separate from the cabin where they sleep, an oil drum has been made into a stove. Gamaliel's aunt Amelia works the dough, or *masa*, on a stone slab called a *metate*. The dough is a mixture of cornmeal that has been soaked in lye to make the paste for the *tortillas*. The paste must be smooth, without lumps. When Aunt Amelia finishes working the mixture, Gamaliel's mother, Rosa María, takes a small handful and puts it into a press that squeezes it flatter than a very thin pancake. She then puts the tortilla on the metal top of the oil drum to cook. Noemi "cooks" on her own little metate. Slap, slap, pat, pat—her little hands push and mash the masa.

For breakfast the children eat their tortillas and drink coffee from thick mugs. Rosa María begins to simmer a pot of mutton stew for their other meal of the day. Amelia stands with her baby in the doorway waiting for her husband, Evodio, to come from Mexico City. Evodio is the oldest son of Juan and Domatilla. He is Gamaliel's uncle. Like Gamaliel's father he must work in Mexico City, where the pay is better and his older children can attend school. When Gamaliel is a teenager he, too, will go to Mexico City to work with his father and uncle and maybe go back to school.

This morning Evodio has finally arrived. He and Amelia and their niece Belon go to the market to buy things for the ofrenda, or offering, they will make for the grandparents. The offering consists of an altar laden with flowers and food and familiar and favorite possessions from the person's life on earth.

Their first stop in the market is the flower vendors. Colorful flowers explode from buckets and are heaped on tables. Amelia buys some *cempasúchil* and then some frothy red blossoms called fer-de-lance, after a type of snake.

Next they stop for fruit and then for several loaves of pan de muerto. At a dry goods store they choose special candles that will burn all night. And for the children they buy chocolate skulls and a chocolate coffin with a sugar skeleton inside.

When they return from the market everyone helps set up the ofrenda in the log house that Juan and Domatilla built. It is in this one-room house that Gamaliel and his mother, sisters, and brothers now sleep. But it is not just a room for sleeping: it is also a room for gathering. Gamaliel's aunt from down the valley comes with her children. Another aunt brings a picture of the parents whose spirits they welcome back.

The late afternoon light slants in through the small windows and narrow door. The air in the room seems spun with gold light. The women speak softly as they arrange the flowers and bread on the table. The children watch from the bed. It is Evodio's honor as the oldest son of Juan and Domatilla to pour some of the tequila his father loved and put it on the table. The women light the candles. Rosa María places the picture of herself with Domatilla on the table.

28

All is ready now. In the small room, the women wrapped in their rebozos speak softly. Everyone remembers the old ones, their parents and grandparents. As the light outside grows dim, umber shadows slide across the floor and the candles cast small halos of honey-colored light over the table.

The next morning every-one prepares to go to the cemetery. The children put on fresh clothes and have their hair brushed. While they are waiting they sit on the front steps eating their chocolate and sugar skulls. They eat them slowly and carefully. Some eat the jaws first and then the sunken cheeks. Others start at the top of the skulls. The older children warn the little ones not to eat the sequins that decorate the eye sockets.

One of Gamaliel's cousins looks into the sky and cries out, *"¡Mariposa! ¡Mariposa!"* He has just spotted the first monarch butterflies from the north. These butterflies ride the warm thermal updrafts over the ridge beyond the far meadows where the sheep graze.

When everyone is ready the family goes to the cemetery. Outside the walls of the cemetery there are ice-cream and flower and fruit vendors. There is a tortilla stand, and soft drinks are sold, too. People arrive with blankets and picnic baskets. But first they go to work on the tumbas.

The grandchildren and children of Juan and Domatilla have brought their hoes and picks and shovels for weeding, and more flowers. It looks as if flowers have suddenly sprouted legs, as small children laden with immense bouquets make their way to the graves.

he graves of Juan and Domatilla are simple dirt mounds with wooden crosses. There are no fancy statues or gravestones. The children and their parents begin pulling up the weeds that have grown up over the past year. They rake and smooth the soil, and in old tin cans sunken into the ground at the corners of the graves they create beautiful flower arrangements.

"¡Aquí está Abuela! ¡Y aquí está Abuelo!" (Here is Grandmother! And here is Grandfather!) Evodio says to one of his small nephews as he takes a few single stems of flowers and sticks them directly into the dirt. After they have tended the graves of Juan and Domatilla, the family goes to a corner of the cemetery where the graves are much smaller. This is where the children and babies are buried. There is a grave for the baby of Evodio and Amelia who died before his first birthday.

The grave is small, and it does not take long to rake and weed and to put the flowers around it. They do not cry while they do this but talk of the flowers and of the picnic they will have when they leave the cemetery. Amelia pats the dirt gently. As she works she whispers to the baby she carries in her shawl to quiet him.

Throughout the cemetery families are busy cleaning up the graves of their loved ones. Some weed dirt mounds like the ones of the de Jesús family. Others scrub and sweep out small stone buildings or crypts. In addition to bringing flowers and candles, people bring fruit and bread to place on the graves. Some bring guitars to play or radios to listen to, for they will spend the entire night in the cemetery.

That evening in the village, children dressed as mummies, ghosts, and ghouls run through the streets shouting, "¡Calaveras! ¡Calaveras!" and hold out boxes or bowls for coins and candies.

As the evening light descends, the candles burn on the tombs and benevolent shadows slide across the night. The darkness drinks the purples and pinks of the flowers, but the bright orange beaks of the bird-of-paradise blossoms stab the night, and the white-throated calla lilies stretching toward the moon catch its light.

44

Gamaliel recalls the day shortly after his abuela died, when his older brother Israel thought he saw her ghost in the market. Israel ran all the way back from the village to their house in the valley to ask his mother if it was true. Had Domatilla really died? And Rosa María said, "What do you mean, 'really'?" She told him not to be scared. The dead only die if they die in our hearts.

Gamaliel thinks his mother is right. He feels his heart pumping. He can remember so clearly tending the sheep with Abuela. He can remember then as if it were now. But perhaps those days were just a dream? Were they more real than now, on this eve of los Días de Muertos, when he feels his abuela's spirit? It seems as if she has never left.

The darkness deepens. The stems of flowers dissolve in the shadows of midnight. The candles flicker in the autumn breeze. A prayer is murmured, a lily trembles in the wind, a few soft chuckles lace the dark as the invisible spirits press closer. Abuela needs no marigold path, Gamaliel thinks. Domatilla is like a butterfly, the monarch: she can always find her way. And then he smiles softly to himself in the darkness.

MORE ABOUT THE DAYS OF THE DEAD CELEBRATION

The **Days of the Dead**, which span the evenings of October 31 through November 2, are not the only holidays that celebrate the spirits of departed ancestors. They are part of a larger tradition in which rites commemorating harvest and death are mixed.

All Saints' Day and **All Souls' Day** are two Christian holidays that grew out of mourning practices such as those celebrated in ancient Egypt and Rome that commemorated the dead. The origin of All Saints' Day, November 1, which was dedicated as a time to pray to all saints, is obscure. It was first celebrated in May, but by the year 800, November 1 was the date observed in honor of both saints as well as martyrs.

In the eleventh century, Odilo, the abbot of the Cluny monastery, dedicated November 2 as the day to remember the souls of baptized Christians who were believed to be in purgatory because they had died with the guilt of sin on their souls. By the thirteenth century All Souls' Day was being celebrated regularly throughout the Christian world.

In medieval England, **All Hallows' Eve** was celebrated on the night of October 31, the night before All Saints' Day. In ancient England, the Celtic festival of **Samhain**, which noted the passing of summer and the return of herds from the pastures, was also observed on this date. It was thought that this was when the souls of the dead revisited their homes. Stories of ghosts, witches, hobgoblins, and cats roaming the countryside were told. People often built huge bonfires on hilltops to frighten evil spirits away. In England there was a custom similar to trick-or-treating called "souling" or "soul-caking." On All Souls' Eve poor people would go about begging currant buns. There was indeed a blending of pagan and Christian beliefs, and gradually Halloween became a secular holiday.

Osiris was the Egyptian god of the dead and also the god of life, vegetation, and fertility. According to an ancient myth, Osiris had been slain by the Egyptian god Seth, who drowned him and then tore his body into fourteen pieces and cast them across the earth. Osiris's wife, Isis, found the pieces and buried them, thus giving new life to the god. Osiris therefore became associated with growth and the promise of new life as much as with death. Osiris festivals in November, at the time of the Nile's annual sinking, became popular throughout Egypt. People would reenact the god's murder by Seth. "Osiris gardens" were constructed. These gardens consisted of a mold in the shape of Osiris that would be filled with soil, then moistened with the water of the Nile and sown with grain. The sprouting grain symbolized the strength and power of the god.

The **Aztecs** were the native people of central Mexico. They are known for their highly developed civilization. Many of their buildings and monuments, including pyramids, still stand. They were conquered in 1521 by Hernán Cortés, an explorer from Spain.

Mictlantecuhtli was the Aztec god of death. He was not feared but rather looked upon as a kind deity who released people from the burdens and harshness of life. There were many Aztec rituals and celebrations surrounding Mictlantecuhtli and the underworld of **Mictlan**, which he ruled. With the Spanish conquest new rituals were introduced, many of which were similar to the Aztec ones. All Saints' Day and All Souls' Day began to blend in seamlessly with the harvest and death rites of Mictlantecuhtli.

Monarch butterflies, whose annual arrival in Mexico coincides with the Days of the Dead celebration, are also known as *Danaus plexippus,* or milkweed butterflies, because their larvae feed on milkweed. Within a year four generations of monarchs are born. Most have life spans of only a few weeks. But the fourth generation, known as the autumn migrant, lives for several months. Those autumn migrants born east of the Rocky Mountains migrate to the oyamel fir forests of central Mexico, which are in a range of transvolcanic mountains. The monarchs west of the Rockies migrate to various sites in California, especially around Monterey.

GLOSSARY

abuela: grandmother

abuelo: grandfather

calacas: handmade Days of the Dead figurines showing skeletons working and playing

calavera: skull

mariposa: butterfly

masa: dough, or the cornmeal mixture used to make tortillas

metate: a flat stone platform used for grinding and pulverizing grains

ofrenda: offering

oyamel: a species of fir tree that grows in the mountain ranges of Mexico and in which monarch butterflies roost during the winter months

pan: bread

rebozo: a woven shawl worn by many Mexican women; they sometimes wrap their babies in a rebozo and carry them by tying the shawl around their shoulders

tortillas: very thin pancakes made from cornmeal; a staple of the Mexican diet, they are used much like bread

tumbas: graves